A Funny Old World

in pictures

Pictures
to share

For Wendy, Jo, Sylv and Sheila,
and a laugh with old friends
on summer days.

**Pictures
to share**

First published in 2008 by
Pictures to Share Community Interest Company,
a UK based social enterprise that publishes
illustrated books for older people.

www.picturestoshare.co.uk

ISBN 978-0-9553940-4-1

Front Cover:	Jack Russell terrier. Photograph by Jo Sax/Stone+/Getty Images
Front endpapers:	Children are fascinated by a man on stilts. Photograph Keystone/Hulton Archive/Getty Images
Back endpapers:	Alaskan Inupiat boy in traditional parka, Photograph by Ken Graham/Stone/Getty Images
Title page:	Two contestants roaring with laughter during a laughing competition on Sandown pier. Hulton Archive/Getty Images
Back cover:	Detail from photograph by Lars Borges/ Photonica/Getty Images Detail from photograph of couple on Sandown Pier (above) Detail from photograph by VCL/Spencer Rowell/Taxi/Getty Images

A Funny Old World

in pictures

Edited by Helen J Bate

Why does it snow?

Why does it snow?
The children come
crowding around me to know.
I said to my nephew,
I said to my niece,
It's just the old woman
a-plucking her geese.

Quotation from 'Why does it Snow?' by Laura E Richards (1850-1943)

Main photograph Kyle George / Aurora / Getty Images Small photograph: Light micrograph
of a snowflake taken by Wilson Bentley (1865-1931). Bentley, a farmer from Vermont, USA,
was the first person to successfully photograph snow flakes, taking the first photograph in 1885.
He used a bellows camera attached to a light microscope. NOAA/SCIENCE PHOTO LIBRARY

I get no kick from champagne

Mere alcohol doesn't thrill me at all
So tell me why should it be true
That I get a kick out of you.

Quotation from song 'I get a kick out of you'
1934 by Cole Porter (1891-1964)

Photograph: A pair of winklepickers 1960.
FPG/Hulton Archive/Getty Images

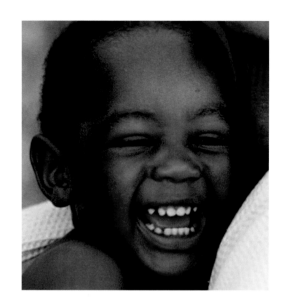

When you're smiling,

When you're smiling,
The whole world smiles with you.

Words from song 'When you're Smiling' by Mark Fisher, Joe Goodwin & Larry Shay
Photograph: Mother and toddler by VCL/Spencer Rowell/Taxi/Getty Images

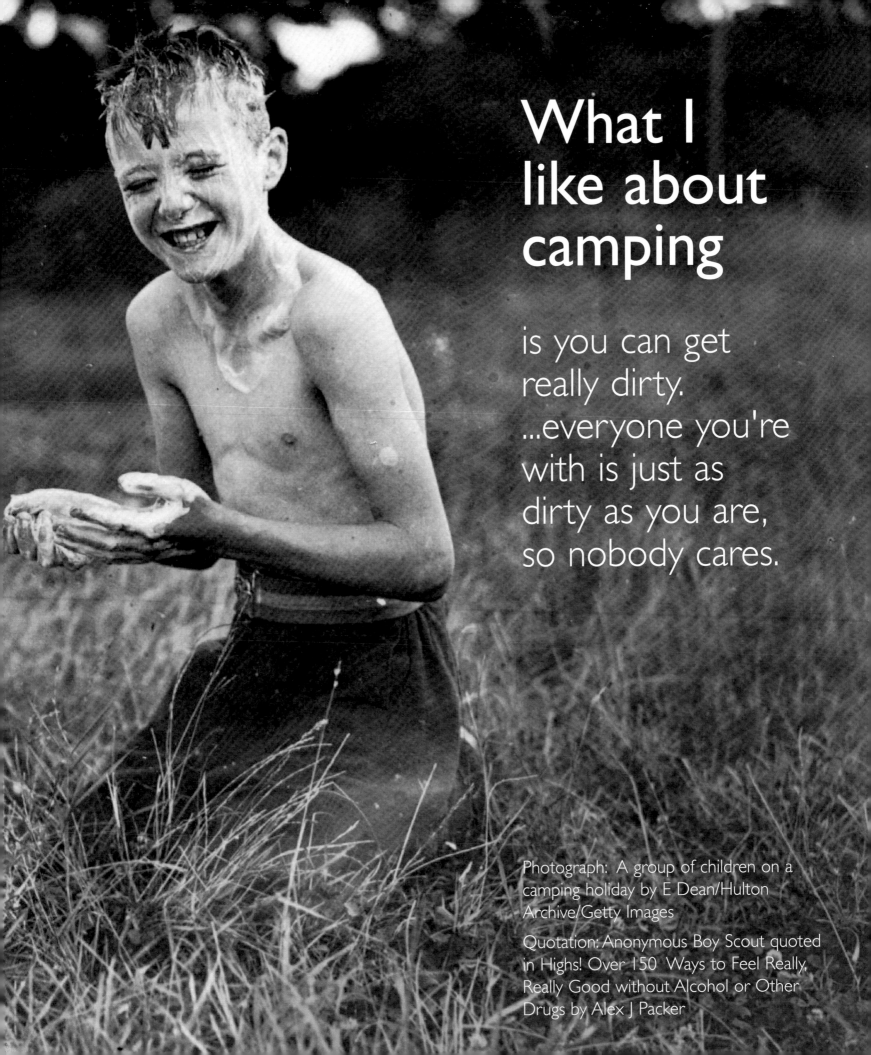

What I like about camping

is you can get
really dirty.
...everyone you're
with is just as
dirty as you are,
so nobody cares.

There's a lion in the living room...

He's gone by morning light;

But every afternoon
He walks right in
and stays all night.

Quotation from song 'Lion In The Living Room' 2005 by
Susan Anders www.songwriter.com/susan/anders.php
Photograph: Lion lying on rug and woman knitting, by
Matthias Clamer/Stone+/Getty Images

Mad dogs and
Englishmen
go out in the midday sun

Quotation from song 'Mad Dogs and Englishmen' written in 1931 by Noel Coward (1899-1973)

Main photograph: Newly wed couples honeymooning in Jersey enjoy some games on the beach. Sack racing is one of the individual events of the day. Haywood Magee/Hulton Archive/Getty Images

Take him

I won't put a price on him.
Take him, he's yours.
Take him, pyjamas look nice on him,
But now he snores!

Quotation from song 'Take Him' 1940 by Lorenz "Larry" Hart (1895-1943)
the lyricist half of the famed Broadway songwriting team Rodgers and Hart.

Photograph: Two women from Rajasthan, India
by Hugh Sitton/Photographer's Choice/Getty Images

Doddy

Photograph of Ken Dodd by Andy Hollingworth reproduced with the permission of Ken Dodd.
Ken Dodd is a well known and popular comedian from Knotty Ash in Liverpool. He was born on the 8th November 1927 and is still performing regularly on stage in 2008 at the age of 81.

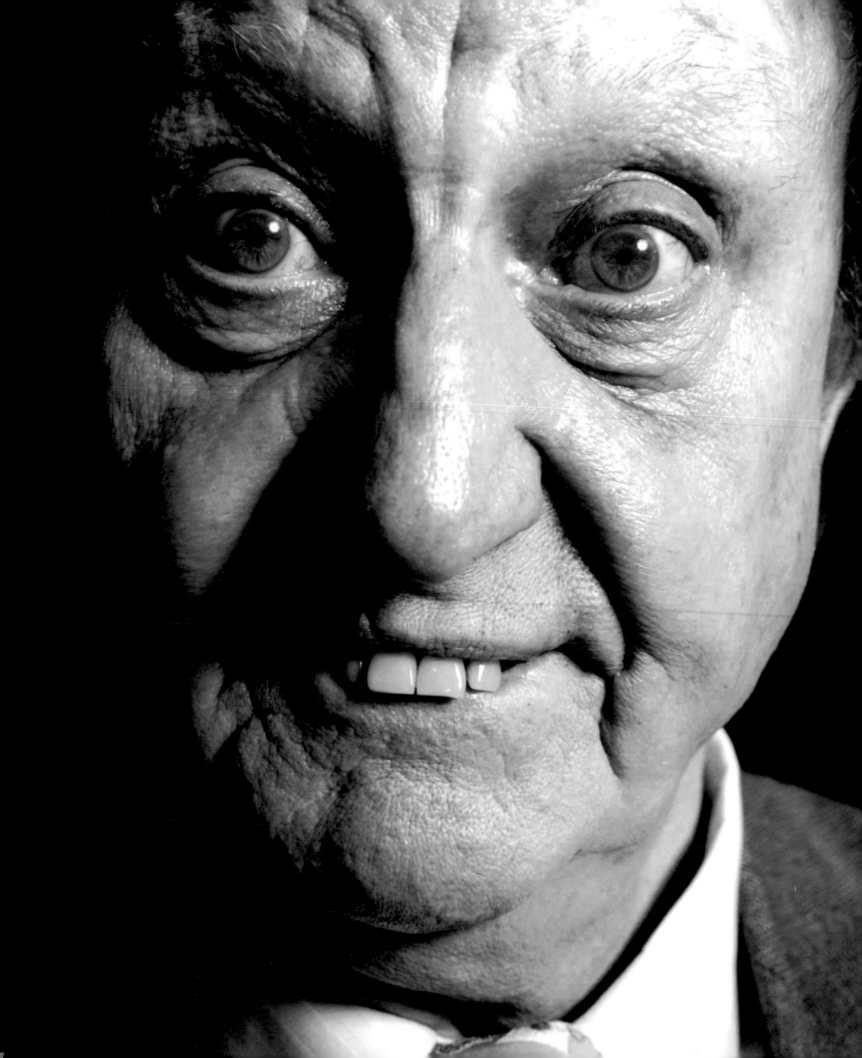

One of the luckiest things

that can happen
to you in life
is to have

a happy childhood

Quotation: Agatha Christie
(1890-1976)
Wit and Wisdom for
the Peanut Butter Gang
H Jackson 1994

Photograph:
Three young monks
sitting at temple,
Sukhothai, Thailand
by Anthony Cassidy
Photographer's
Choice/Getty Images

Now it's a job
that just suits me,

A window cleaner you would be,
If you could see what I can see
When I'm cleanin' windows!

Text from song 'When I'm Cleanin' Windows by George Formby (1904-1961)

Photograph: Mind The Ladder. Teun de Vries and Jaap Koevoets use the ladder for
their window cleaning business in the small village of Noordwijk, in Holland, and carry
the ladder on their bicycles. Photo by Harry Kerr/Hulton Archive/Getty Images

Why did the chicken cross the road?

Photograph:
A chicken crossing the road
by Christian Michaels/
Taxi/Getty Images

You can teach an elephant to dance,

but the likelihood of it stepping on your toes is very high.

Photograph: An Indian elephant with a 'For Sale' sign attached to its tail, circa 1930.
Photo by FPG/Hulton Archive/Getty Images
Quotation: Gary Moss, US marketing coach quoted in Forbes 15th March 1993

Bring me sunshine,

in your smile,
Bring me laughter,
all the while

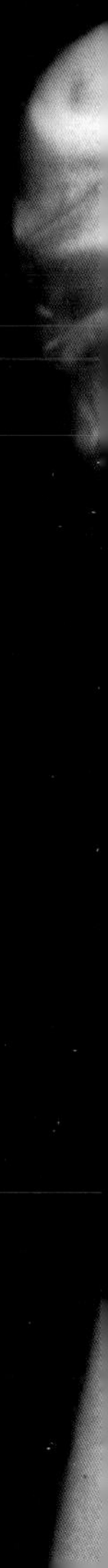

Quotation from Morecambe and Wise signature tune
'Bring me Sunshine' Lyrics by Jack Greene

Photograph: Morecambe & Wise. Fremantle Media
Reproduced with the permission of Billy Marsh Associates
on behalf of the Morecambe & Wise estates

Talent wins games, but

teamwork

wins championships.

Photograph: Man holding large rabbit and trophy by Lars Borges/Photonica/Getty Images

Quotation: Attributed to Michael Jordan, US basketball player

Pictures to share

Acknowledgements

Our thanks to the contributors who have allowed their text or imagery to be used for a reduced or no fee. Thanks also to all those who assisted in the development of this book by helping with or taking part in trials.

All efforts have been made to contact copyright holders. If you own the copyright for work that is represented, but have not been contacted, please get in touch via our website.

Thanks to our sponsors

ANDREWS CHARITABLE TRUST

Some quotations have been provided by 'Chambers Dictionary of Quotations', Chambers Harrap Publishers Ltd, 2005 and www.quotegarden.com

Published by

Pictures to Share Community Interest Company.
Peckforton, Cheshire
www.picturestoshare.co.uk

Printed in England by
Langham Press, Station Road, Foxton
Cambridgeshire CB22 6SA